Is for Dragon Dance

shì wǔ lóng

是舞龙

by

Ying Chang Compestine

illustrated by

YongSheng Xuan

HOLIDAY HOUSE · NEW YORK

To my dragons, Greg and Vinson
—Y. C. C.

To my little friend Li Rui Jun
—Y. X.

 is for Acrobat

shì zá jì yì rén

是杂技艺人

B is for Balls
shì gǔn qiú
是滚球

Acrobats are flexible and strong. They are masters of balance. People watch them to celebrate the coming of the New Year.

zá jì yì rén shēn tǐ róu rèn yòu qiáng zhuàng dōu shì píng héng dà shī
杂技艺人身体柔韧又强壮，都是平衡大师。

rén men guān kàn zá shuǎ yǎn chū lái qìng zhù xīn nián de dào lái
人们观看杂耍演出来庆祝新年的到来。

C is for Calligraphy
shì chūn lián
是春联

Let's write the characters for "good luck."
(Don't get the ink on your new clothes!)

ràng wǒ mén yì qǐ shū xiě rú yì
让我们一起书写「如意」。

bié ràng mò shuǐ nòng zāng le xīn yī fu
(别让墨水弄脏了新衣服!)

D is for Dragon Dance

shì wǔ lóng

是舞龙

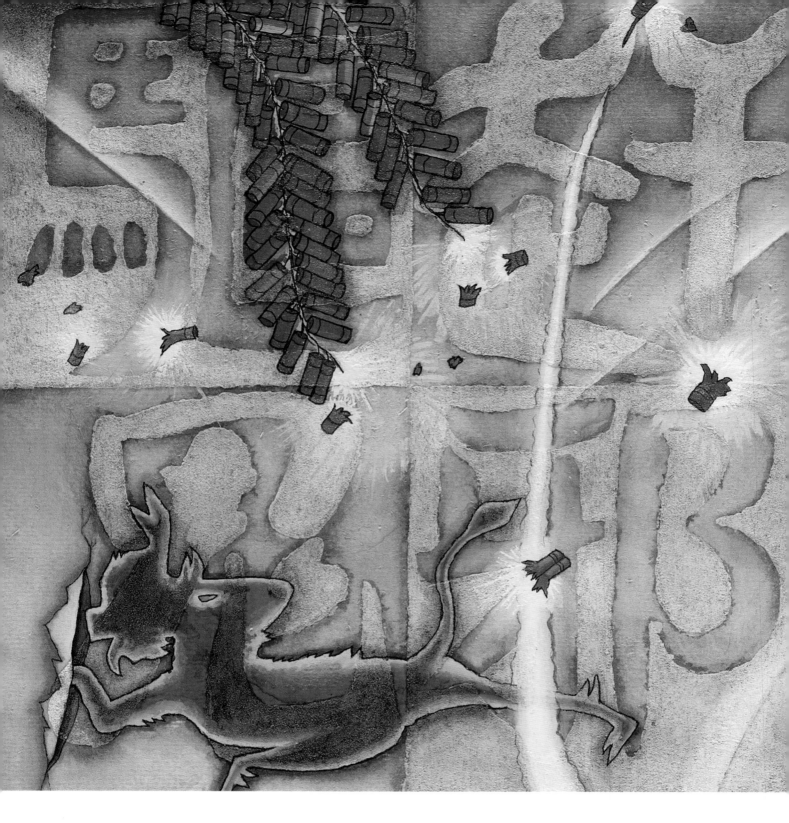

 **is for Evil Spirits**
shì guǐ guài
是鬼怪

 F is for Firecrackers
shì biān pào
是 鞭 炮

Dragon dancers and firecrackers
scare away evil spirits.

wǔ lóng rén hé biān pào shēng xià zǒu guǐ guài
舞龙人和鞭炮声吓走鬼怪。

G

is for Grandma and Grandpa
shì yé ye nǎi nai
是爷爷奶奶

Grandma and Grandpa decorate their home with traditional cut paper and calligraphy to honor the New Year.

yé ye nǎi nai yòng chuán tǒng jiǎn zhǐ hé chūn lián
爷爷奶奶用传统剪纸和春联
bǎ jiā zhuāng shì qǐ lái gōng hè xīn chūn
把家装饰起来恭贺新春。

H is for Haircut
shì lǐ fà
是理发

Children get their hair washed and cut, and put on new clothes for a fresh start in the New Year.

hái zǐ men xǐ tóu lǐ fà huàn shàng xīn yī shang qī dài xīn nián de xīn kāi shǐ
孩子们洗头理发换上新衣裳，期待新年的新开始。

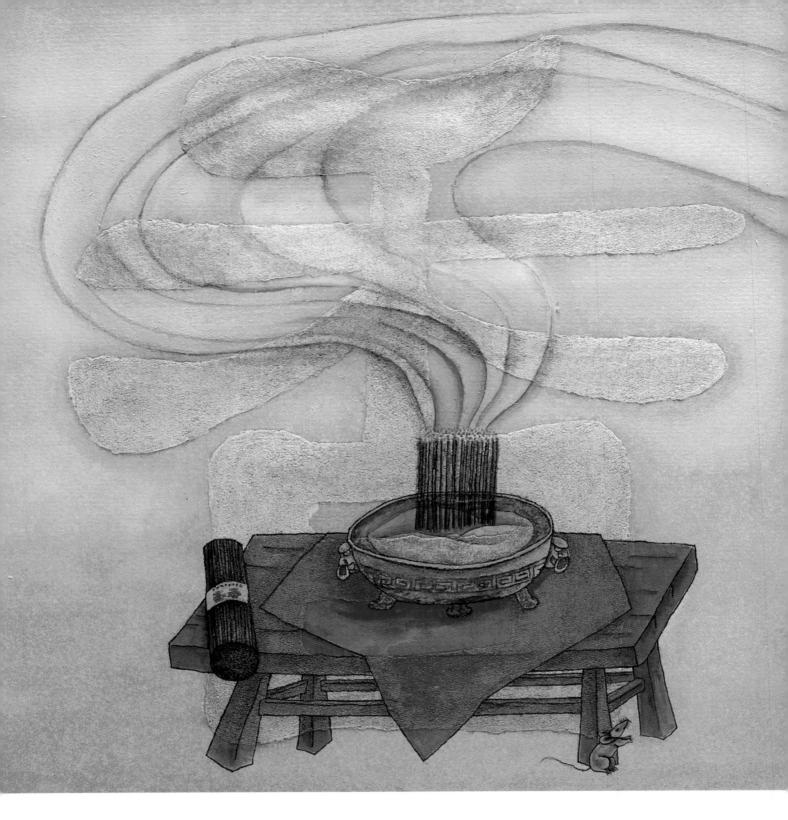

I is for Incense
shì xiāng huǒ
是香火

J is for Jade
shì yù shí
是玉石

Chinese people burn incense and wear jade to protect themselves from evil.

zhōng guó rén diǎn xiāng huǒ dài yù shí lái pì xié
中国人点香火、戴玉石来辟邪。

 is for Kites

shì fēng zhēng

是风筝

L is for Lanterns
shì dēng long
是灯笼

Chinese people believe that flying kites and lantern light scare away evil spirits.

zhōng guó rén xiāng xìn fēi wǔ de fēng zhēng hé dēng long de guāng néng
中国人相信飞舞的风筝和灯笼的光

xià zǒu guǐ guài
能吓走鬼怪

M is for Moon
shì yuè liàng
是月亮

Chinese New Year starts with a new moon.

zhōng guó xīn nián suí xīn yuè kāi shǐ
中国新年随新月开始。

N is for Noodle
shì miàn tiáo
是面条

Eat noodles for a long, happy life.

chī miàn tiáo xiàng zhēng zhe cháng shòu xìng fú de yì shēng
吃面条象征着长寿、幸福的一生。

 O is for Oranges
shì jú zi
是橘子

Bring oranges to your friends' houses.
They represent good fortune.

dài shàng jú zi qù bài fǎng péng yǒu jú zi xiàng zhēng zhe hǎo yùn
带上橘子去拜访朋友。橘子象征着好运。

P is for Peking Duck
shì běi jīng kǎo yā
是北京烤鸭

A whole roasted duck means happiness.

kǎo quán yā xiàng zhēng zhe xìng fú
烤全鸭象征着幸福。

 **is for Quiz**
shì dēng mí
是灯谜

Solve the tricky quiz and you may win a big prize.

jiě kāi qiǎo miào de dēng mí nǐ jiù néng dé dào dà jiǎng
解开巧妙的灯谜，你就能得到大奖。

R is for Red Envelopes
shì hóng bāo
是红包

Children receive red envelopes that contain good-luck money.

hái zi men huì shōu dào zhuāng zhe yā suì qián de hóng bāo
孩子们会收到装着压岁钱的红包。

S is for Steamed Dumplings
shì zhēng jiǎo
是蒸饺

Eat these special treats to begin the New Year.

chī chūn jié tè sè zhēng jiǎo lái yíng xīn nián
吃春节特色蒸饺来迎新年！

T is for Tradition
shì chuán tǒng
是传统

Chinese people all over the world follow similar New Year's traditions.

quán qiú huá rén dōu àn zhe xiāng sì de chuán tǒng xí sú guò nián
全球华人都按着相似的传统习俗过年。

U is for Unity

shì tuán yuán

是团圆

Chinese families unite for the New Year's feast.

zhōng guó jiā tíng zài xīn nián yì qǐ chī tuán yuán fàn

中国家庭在新年一起吃团圆饭。

V is for Veneration
shì bài zǔ
是拜祖

Families venerate their ancestors at New Year's.

zài xīn nián quán jiā rén yì qǐ bài zǔ xiān
在新年，全家人一起拜祖先。

 **is for Wish**
shì zhù fú
是祝福

The New Year is a time to give good wishes.

xīn nián shì dà jiā xiāng hù zhù fú de rì zǐ
新年是大家相互祝福的日子。

X is for Xylograph

shì mù diāo
是木雕

Wood carvings on the doors keep out evil spirits.

mén shàng de mù diāo jù guǐ guài yú mén wài
门上的木雕拒鬼怪于门外。

Y is for Yo-Yos

shì kōng zhú
是 空 竹

New Year's is a good time to play. Chinese yo-yos fly so high, they might reach the sky.

xīn nián shì wán shuǎ de hǎo rì zǐ kōng zhú fēi dé gāo sì hū néng tiān
新年是玩耍的好日子空竹飞得高，似乎能碰到天。

Z is for Zodiac

shì shí èr shēng xiào

是十二生肖

The Chinese calendar follows a twelve-year cycle. Each year is represented by a different animal. Do you know the sign for your birth year?

zhōng guó de jì nián yǐ shí èr nián wéi yì xún huán
中国的纪年以十二年为一循环，
měi yí gè dòng wù dài biǎo qí zhōng yì nián nǐ zhī dào nǐ de shǔ xiàng ma
每一个动物代表其中一年。你知道你的属相吗？

Author's Note

The Chinese lunar calendar is based on the phases of the moon and follows a twelve-year cycle, with each year represented by a different animal. Traditions for the New Year are carefully followed during the celebration, which lasts for fifteen days. The most important part of the festivities—the New Year parades—feature dancing dragons, symbols of goodness and strength.

Tips to Ensure Good Fortune in the New Year

Clean: Tidy up and clean the house before the New Year starts. You don't want to sweep out your good fortune on New Year's Day. Get rid of old, unused items to make room for the new.

Get a Haircut: This lets everyone know you are ready for a fresh start this New Year.

Wear New Clothes: Dress in new clothes so the evil spirits won't recognize you in the New Year.

Collect Li-Shih or Red Envelopes: Children bow to elders to show their respect. In return, they are given red envelopes that contain money for prosperity in the year ahead.

Fire Away: Firecrackers frighten away evil spirits and welcome the New Year.

Meet and Greet: Visit friends and relatives and exchange treats and fruit with one another. Oranges and tangerines are said to bring health and wealth in the New Year.

Eat Dumplings: They symbolize happiness, wealth, and family togetherness.

Artist's Note

You may notice the Chinese characters that appear in the background of each page of this book. They use four different calligraphic styles:

龍 is "Dragon" from the Song dynasty

龍 is "Dragon" from the Wei dynasty

龙 is "Dragon" in the Grass style ("cursive" characters)

龍 is "Dragon" from the Han dynasty

On some pages the characters make up Chinese sayings; on others they represent a single word.

Special thanks to Carrie Reed, Associate Professor of Chinese at Middlebury College, and Belinda Chan, professional translator, for their expertise and assistance.

Text copyright © 2006
by Ying Chang Compestine

Illustrations copyright © 2006
by YongSheng Xuan

Simplified Chinese translation copyright © 2018 by Ying Compestine and Xinyang Chen

Bilingual typography & design
by Chun-wo Pat,
Whitespace Integrated Design, Inc.

The Library of Congress has catalogued the prior edition as follows:
Compestine, Ying Chang.
D is for dragon dance/
by Ying Chang Compestine ;
illustrated by YongSheng Xuan.
p. cm.
ISBN 0-8234-1887-1
1. Chinese New Year—Juvenile literature.
1. Xuan, YongSheng, ill. II. Title.
GT4905. C65 2005
394.261—dc22
2004058139

ISBN 978-0-8234-4029-0 (bilingual edition)

Visit our website for an exclusive and delicious New Year's dumpling recipe from cooking show host and former *Martha Stewart Living* editor Ying Chang Compestine!

HolidayHouse.com